OUT OF MY MIND
A Symphony of Essays, Writings, and Poems

BY
Mary Ellen Lisciandra
Illustrated by Chris Pritchett
Edited by Matt Marshal

Enjoy my book
Merry Christmas
Mary Ellen Lisciandra

ISBN 978-1-61225-430-2

Published by Mirror Publishing
Fort Payne, Alabama 35967

Printed in the USA.

Dedicated to Cairo -- My best friend ever.

<u>To The Improvement of Morals and Values</u>

Man -- What are you after all?
An evil, corrupt, courageous, inventive animal
that has no equal on earth.
And yes -- more beautiful; and even at times, more humane.

INTRODUCTION

Let me tell you a story, some poems,
and, perhaps, indulge in a little bit of
fantasy, mirth, and quiet reflection.

These writings are really needed in today's
world. So I give you a haunting escape,
mixed with very powerful consequences.

There was always a price to pay for our
actions. But at the same time, we must
always maintain a sense of compassion. I
believe that if we can keep a balance
between these two forces, we might be able
to achieve the happiness that we all strive
to attain in a less than perfect world.

I want my works to be read with thought,
and with a delighted awareness of style.

My hope is that my readers will enjoy the
style and versatility of my writing, while still
holding their values and convictions.

Some people find wisdom with age; but
others need to change their lives.

THE GREAT SOCIETY

It was a time of war.
It was a time of peace.
Demonstrations raged over the land.
Hate toward your brother;
While at war with another --
Yet this nation was giving a hand.

Some campaign funds are usually spent
    in a more unscrupulous way.
The money they sought
    was spent with one thought --
Giving them pleasures day by day.

Now taxes get bigger every year,
    and your salary dwindles down so low.
Taxes for this;
Taxes for that --
Yet you still wonder where they really go.

Yes --
We were all but pawns,
    you and me --
Products of The Great Society.

They come to me when I'm sleeping,
    or lying half awake.
Into my subconscious;
    these dreams take many a shape.

Is it the way I really feel:
    both morbid and prettily seen?
Flights of fancy, hate,
    or thinking myself unclean.

Should I dare tell them to someone?
Or repress them with locked key?
Yes – I'll keep them carefully hidden;
    so no one else can see.

But now the night is coming,
    and with it my so-called rest.
Will I sleep in undisturbed slumber?
Or will my mind be put to the test?

My dreams are coming.
I can see them now --
    ready to escape.
I lay powerless to hold them back --
    fearful, guilty, happy to partake.

It is all over.
They have made their hasty retreat.
Locked in my subconscious;
    waiting 'til next time we meet.

A DAY FOR ALL SEASONS

May is for our mothers.
And in June, there's no question about
    tributes to our fathers.
But this is not what I'm writing about.

A special day should be set aside --
    I think it's only fair --
Dedicated to our grandparents,
    in equal grandiose flair.

They sit silently in the background,
    bearing the loneliness they feel --
Trying desperately to reach us;
    uttering their words with zeal.

So is it our generations
    that bridge us so far apart?
Or do we forget they're people, too --
    complete with a heart?

The moral, dear friends, lies deeper
    in this poem I wrote.
For their day is a day for all seasons --
A day for a special kind of folk.

LIES

It doesn't take long before you eventually find out
    certain so-called truths you cherished so devout.

And then the pain, to see them crumble beneath your feet –
Washed away like dirt down some lonely street.

Your thoughts are so confused;
For you have been slighted and abused.

The rage you feel is real;
The tears you can't conceal.

And your fist clinched ever so tight.
Should you run; or should you fight?

The pros and cons are weighed.
A decision must soon be made.

Now a fool will immediately take to flight --
Mulling over his tales of woe, both day and night.

But the man who stays learns his lesson well --
Making it his goal, before he dies,
    never to destroy anyone with cancerous lies.

ALONE

The beautiful people are gone,
    and there you sit alone.
Emptiness and tears come easy,
    when you are alone.

There is no one who will listen,
    with a sympathetic ear.
No one to share your precious memories --
    even if they aren't real.

"Who cares?" you ask.
"Who cares!" you shout.
But no one answers.

You are not realistic;
    for you live in the past.
You have the world at your feet.
Now . . .
Gone forever.

Oh -- if I could only do it all over again,
    it would be different.
But you can't.

Life slips away,
    and here you are --
Stuck in this crummy apartment;
Old and alone.

MY ROOM

Pretty things fill my room;
But then again, it needs the broom.

An unmade bed in which I sprawl --
Close to the television by the wall.

Blouses and skirts drape every chair --
With the radio blasting.
Come in, if you dare.

A welcome retreat, in which I have peace --
To think my own thoughts,
    where dreams never cease.

So if I'm unhappy, depressed and with gloom --
I can always depend on that faithful friend,
    which I call my room.

THE GAMBLE

I dreamed that I was walking down a long and winding road.
All was quite well enough, it seemed --
Mind free, with no heavy load.

Then it happened --
For it appeared the road split in two:
One to the right;
One to the left.
Now what was I to do?

The road on the left was filled with much gay fantasy;
Tempting me with promises,
    and images of what life would be to me.

But the road on the right showed me joys, sorrow,
    people of both good and ill repute;
Promising me nothing as I sat,
    deciding to choose my route.

The path I chose was the one facing left,
    and I have travelled it many years.
My glorious dreams of grandeur trampled --
Complete with letdowns and tears.

I yearned and prayed that if I could,
    I would find that other road.
It mattered oh so much to me;
Until one day,
    I turned around and faced reality.

TURTLE TRIVIA

In the religions of various peoples, the turtle is venerated as a sacred animal. In pre-classical civilizations, turtles were already considered the symbol of prudence and intelligence. A number of small statues with turtle motifs can be found in the countries of Eastern Asia.

Every day, the shape of the turtle is found in a wide variety of places: as the trademark of various firms, on stamps, labels in catalogs, posters, coats of arms, coins, and a funny television commercial.

Finally, the turtle plays a considerable part in fairy tales, myths, and legends. The folklore of Native Americans is particularly rich in turtle stories.

It is hoped that, in the future, a friendly attitude of the turtle by people will contribute to the conservation of healthy, protected oceans, with wild and flourishing ecosystems, and filled with diverse and abundant wildlife.

GETTYSBURG

As we walked through the gates of the National Cemetery, our tour group became quiet. Even the children knew this place was special.

The grass, no longer stained with the blood of fallen comrades, retained its lush, green colors for another year. Stately oak trees, with their massive trunks centuries old -- the last remaining witnesses of the great battle -- seemed oblivious to our presence. Here they stood – living monuments -- guarding their memories for all time.

It was here – among these peaceful surroundings, farms, and bright summer landscapes – that the victorious army of Northern Virginia, under the command of General Robert E. Lee, would once and for all defeat the army of the Potomac.

The North, still reeling from the stinging defeat of Chancellorsville, was now under the command of George Mead. The stakes were high, as men and horses screamed, while being blown apart by deadly cannon and mini balls.

The smell of rotting flesh filled the air against the blistering July sun. Across the open field, the bullet-riddled colors of Old Glory, and the bonnie-blue flag of the South, floated in the sunlight over the corpses and scattered limbs of these brave men.

After three days, the battle ended with a much-needed victory for the North. Forty-three thousand casualties rest in the silent graves on Cemetery Hill. These men, who fought so valiantly for their cause, are now forever honored in their final resting place:

This hallowed ground – Gettysburg.

THE YEAR GOD BECAME
A METS FAN

Here is a story of a baseball team,
    which you may not believe;
And of the many countless fans,
    whose courage did not leave.

After the Dodgers had left New York,
    amid a tearful plea;
Could there be a team to replace sadness
    with a little spark of glee?

So God looked down and heard our prayers,
    rising higher than all the great sunsets;
And said "Not only will they have a team;
They'll be known as the New York Mets."

But alas, the Mets were losers --
Clowns for seven years;
The stumble bums of baseball --
Casey Stengel's hapless dears.

So Casey left as manager,
    replaced by a man named Gil --
Determined to make them winners,
    with fortitude and will.

As if by magic, the Mets did rise
    to an unbelieving number two.
In a see-saw battle they dethroned the Cubs --
Leaving them black and blue.

The "Amazing Mets," -- as they now were called --
    swept Atlanta: One - Two - Three.
And now they had to face a team
    assured of victory.

The team was the mighty Orioles --
Picked as the World Series winner.
"We'll club them in four! And if we're still sore,
    we'll have each Met for dinner."

So it all began in Baltimore,
    and the first round had begun.
Although the Mets tried hard, they lost the game;
And granted the Birds had won.

What happened now, for the next four games;
No one can explain
    how the Mets defeated the birds --
And won their way to fame.

All of a sudden, there came a change
    in game number two.
As if powered by an unknown force,
    they left Baltimore's fans stunned and blue.

The birds then boasted:
"We'll beat them with ease."
But into Shea Stadium -- gone unnoticed --
Flowed this gentle breeze.

Some say there were angels in the outfield --
Not merely just a man.
And some even say it was truly because
God was a great Met fan.

Call it luck.
Call it baseball.
Call it whatever you please.
But can you explain why Cleon Jones
    dropped humbly to his knees?

So, this is the story of the champion Mets --
Winners all to the very last man.
Just ask any Baltimorean,
    if God isn't a great Mets fan.

A VISIT FROM KING DICK

Twas the night before Christmas,
    and all through the house;
Not an oil burner stirring,
    while I shivered in my blouse.

So we huddled together,
    by the chimney with care;
In hopes that King Dick
    soon would be there.

The children were frozen
    all stiff in their beds;
While visions of oil drops
    danced in their heads.

And me, wrapped in blankets,
    and Father, too;
Hoping and praying
    we don't all catch the flu.

When out on the lawn
    there arose such a clatter.
I sprang from my electric blanket,
    to see what was the matter.

The floor was like ice,
    as I quick grabbed my gun.
Another log poacher
    out on the run?

Yes -- every house guarded
    their precious supply;
With barbed-wire fences
    nearly reaching the sky.

When what to my wandering eyes
    should appear --
But a golden throne,
    and eight tiny reindeer.

With a little old driver
    so tricky and slick;
I knew in a moment,
    it must be King Dick.

More rapid he came --
    like an old whipper-snapper;
With new proclamation:
    "Operation Linebacker."

As I drew in my head
    and was turning around;
Down the chimney King Dick
    came with a bound.

"No oil, this Christmas?" I asked,
    getting up nerve.
"No oil!" he bellowed.
    "You must conserve."

His eyes how they gleamed,
    while looking at me.
His cheeks were jowls;
    his nose -- ski.

He had a grin on his face,
    and a little round belly.
When asked about tapes,
    shook like a bowl full of jelly.

Laying five fingers
    aside of his nose;
And giving a nod,
    up the chimney he rose.

He sprang to his throne –
    To his team, gave a whistle.
And away they all flew,
    like a guided missile.

But I heard him exclaim,
    'ere he drove out of sight:
"Hope you don't freeze
    your ass off tonight!"

Now all the dolphins, birds, and fish
    have a sad tale for all to hear.
They cannot stop this mighty sludge --
    destroying everything that's dear.

A real environmental mess
    that's creeping slowly to your dock.
A real environmental mess --
    Yeah Mon, We dance the BP Rock.

How Low Can You Go?

Both man and beast are mighty hot;
    the pristine beaches all but shot.
No one knows what the hell to do --
    an eco-system steeped in goo.

Our waters all but ruined;
    the manatees in shock.
Our waters all but ruined --
    Yeah Mon, We dance the BP Rock.

How Low Can You Go?

Respect the waters and the Earth.
    It was here before your birth.
Now who is next on the list?
    What will it take to resist?

We have to stand up for once,
    and give greed a good, clean sock.
We have to stand up for once --
    Or else we'll dance the BP Rock.

CPSIA information can be obtained
at www.ICGtesting.com
Printed in the USA
BVHW021346030820
585343BV00002B/43

9 781612 254302